Detox
Waters

Detox
Waters

Géraldine Olivo

80 simple
infusions for
health and vitality

PHOTOGRAPHY BY MYRIAM GAUTHIER-MOREAU

quadrille

CONTENTS

WHAT IS
A DETOX?

The word 'detox' (short for detoxification) describes a process that the body performs in order to rid itself of waste products and toxins – including, for example, those toxic substances present in our food (pesticides in fruit and vegetables, heavy metals in fish, scorched fats in BBQ meals) or in the wider environment (pollutants, stress). The toxins we ingest are stored mainly in the body's fat cells. Someone who is overweight is therefore mathematically at greater risk of storing such toxins than someone who is not.

The term 'detox' is often associated with slimming, cleansing or even fasting. In actual fact, the process of detoxification is performed mainly by the liver, which acts as the body's true 'waste-disposal plant'. To function efficiently, the liver needs antioxidants, especially vitamins A, C and E, but also vitamins D, B9 and B12, zinc, selenium, sulphur, omegas 3 and 6, and also proteins.

HOW TO
DETOX

Going on a crash detox course lasting just a few days or weeks is of limited health benefit. It's more valuable to take a broader and closer look at the food you eat all year round. After all, while a couple of weeks of detox following Christmas and the New Year doubtless achieves some short-term positive effects, it can hardly offset the damage caused by poor eating habits during the other fifty weeks of the year!

Luckily, all the compounds that the liver requires to function effectively can be found in an ordinary well-balanced diet. Fruit and vegetables are stuffed with antioxidants and contain plenty of minerals. Omega 3s and 6s are present in the fats in nuts and seeds (walnuts, almonds, sunflower, flax, sesame) and also in animal fats (oily fish, such as mackerel, are rich in Omega 3s). Finally, one shouldn't miss out on protein, which once again can either be derived from animal products (meat, fish, eggs) or vegetable based (pulses, oils, soya). Vitamin B12, on the other hand, can be found only in animal products (especially fish, seafood and offal).

Other than the food one eats, careful attention should be paid to lifestyle and environment. A stressful day-to-day life, an over-polluted atmosphere, a shortfall in physical activity, and sources of conflict and anxiety can be at least as toxic as the worst mass-produced junk food. Giving oneself some quiet downtime, participating in sport or spending a while in the countryside can have a powerful detoxifying effect.

THE BENEFITS OF
DETOX WATERS

As you may imagine, the detox waters featured in this book are not to be thought of as magic potions. They are a vitamin-boosted versions of the water we drink every day and, at the same time, a refreshing and healthy alternative to the various fizzy drinks on the market. But they should always be consumed as part of a balanced diet.

While not all antioxidants are hydrosoluble – which means they dissolve in water during the maceration or steeping process – a great many are.

The main liposoluble antioxidants – those that dissolve in fat – are known as carotenoids. It is carotenoids that give fruit and vegetables their orangey or reddish colour and they are present in the flesh of vegetables even following maceration. To take full advantage of their health benefits, they must ideally be consumed along with some healthy fats, such as a handful of almonds.

The beneficial effects of detox waters are further optimized by the inclusion of a variety of herbs, whose medicinal properties are outlined in the introductions to the recipes.

WHEN TO DRINK
DETOX WATERS

It is preferable to drink detox waters in between meals, especially if a large volume of liquid (such as a big glassful or more) is to be consumed. It is also a good idea to drink a detox water on waking up in the morning, thereby gently reviving the body after a night of complete fasting.

CHOOSING THE RIGHT
FRUIT AND VEGETABLES

Whatever fruit or vegetables you choose to consume, in order to obtain the best results in terms of both taste and health benefits they should be ripe, in season and, importantly, organic. Remember that the fruit and vegetables used in detox waters are not peeled and it is the skin of fruit and vegetables that is most exposed to pesticides. You don't want your detox water to be a marinade of chemicals!

It is best to use fruits that are fresh and locally sourced or, even better, used immediately after they are picked (for example, apples, pears and strawberries). Failing this, from time to time you can use frozen fruits, which are usually of good quality and are frozen straight after they're harvested. Frozen raspberries and melon balls can come in useful when making detox waters.

DOS AND DON'TS
FOR DETOX WATERS

USING BITTER FRUITS OR PLANTS

Be aware of the bitterness of the ingredients you use, which will increase with a lengthy maceration time. Any bitterness can be offset by combining the ingredient either with something acidic (such as lemon or hibiscus) or with sweeter ingredients (such as very ripe soft fruit or dried fruit). Avoid combining fruits or plants that are naturally bitter, for example rosemary with poor-quality green tea, or grapefruit with dandelion. When using citrus fruits or pomegranate seeds, take care to remove all the peel, pith and membranes.

INFUSING SPICES

Do not leave spices (such as sticks of cinnamon, cloves, cardamom pods, vanilla pods) to macerate whole. In order for their flavours to infuse well they must be crushed.

CHOOSING VEGETABLES

The few vegetables included in the recipes have been chosen either for their pleasant taste (celery, fennel) or their slightly sweet taste (carrot, parsnip). Despite their health benefits, certain vegetables are not suitable for use in detox waters. This applies to cabbage, broccoli, potatoes and turnips.

USING NUTS

Antinutrients are contained in the fine skins that envelop nuts, such as almonds and hazelnuts. In order to remove at least a proportion of these antinutrients, simply soak the nuts in water for several hours, disposing of the water afterwards. However, if nuts are soaked repeatedly in this way, they will not sufficiently flavour a detox water.

COMBINING FLAVOURS

Avoid combining fruits or vegetables whose flavours are not particularly strong (such as cucumber, pomegranate, watermelon). Or, if you do, make sure to add a more flavorsome ingredient for extra seasoning – for example, a spice, an aromatic herb or a strong-tasting fruit.

A CLOSER LOOK
AT INGREDIENTS

CITRUS FRUIT

Rich in water-soluble vitamin C, oranges, grapefruit, clementines and mandarins make a detox water more refreshing and tangy. To avoid the bitterness of the white pithy membrane that surrounds the pulp, oranges and grapefruit must be thoroughly peeled using a sharp knife so that only the fruit inside is used in the maceration. Clementines and mandarins can be peeled normally.

SOFT FRUIT

Rich in antioxidants, these are easy to use and provide lots of colour. As a general rule, for maximum flavour, soft fruit should be as fresh as possible.

GREEN TEA

Green tea – with its wealth of antioxidants that is more plentiful than in ordinary 'black' tea – can be used to make a super-healthy version of the popular iced-tea drink. Choose quality organic green tea, loose rather than in tea bags, to avoid excessive bitterness.

AROMATIC PLANTS AND HERBS

Whether used fresh or in herbal tea bags, aromatic plants and herbs possess health-giving properties that can be extracted either cold through maceration or hot in an infusion. Place them in either a muslin sachet or a tea ball in order to avoid mixing them with the pieces of fruit or vegetable, which you may wish to eat later on.

SPICES

Cinnamon, cloves, pepper and other spices can act as stimulants to aid digestion or warm the body. Buy them whole rather than ground, then crush them in a mortar immediately before macerating or infusing. This will preserve their properties and prevent them from tasting stale.

ESSENTIAL INFORMATION
BEFORE YOU START

GENERAL PRINCIPLES

All the recipes produce one litre of liquid and should ideally be prepared in the evening for the following day; the resulting drink should be consumed within a maximum of 24 hours. The water used must always be of good quality, either bottled spring water or jug-filtered. Be sure to avoid tap water. When serving, if the jar or bottle is not already fitted with a filter, use a strainer if required.

CONTAINERS

Containers should be made of glass (certainly not plastic). Ideally, use a large glass jar or bottle fitted with a screwtop. Always choose a container larger than one litre, so that it will easily hold the litre of water plus the macerating fruit or vegetables.

CUTTING UP THE INGREDIENTS

Cut up the fruit and vegetables in small enough pieces to allow their flavours and properties to be well infused in the water but not so small that the softer fruits (pear, banana) simply disintegrate. If the fruit is naturally too small to be sliced (berries, for example), crush it gently in a mortar before putting it in the water.

LEMON JUICE

Lemon is added to most recipes, since the antioxidant powers of the vitamin C contained in lemons helps conserve the macerating fruits and vegetables.

SPARKLING WATER

If you so wish, there is nothing to prevent you replacing some of the spring water with sparkling water. Use approximately one half measure of still water to macerate the fruits or vegetables, then add sparkling water to serve. You can opt for a water high in bicarbonate, making sure that it is not too salty (containing too much sodium). This will allow you to benefit from its alkalizing properties.

COOLING

DETOX WATERS

Adding homemade ice cubes will make your glass of detox water all the more appealing and refreshing, while also boosting its detox potential (see recipes on page 122.)

SOFT FRUIT ICE CUBES

Soft fruit provides not only flavonoids but also water-soluble vitamin C, whose antioxidant properties help to conserve the drink. Blueberries are ideal. Whenever possible, choose wild rather than cultivated blueberries: they're smaller, juicier and sweeter smelling.

ALMOND MILK OR COCONUT MILK ICE CUBES

Lipid-rich almond milk and coconut milk promote the absorption of carotenoids contained in most fruit and orange-coloured vegetables.

TEA OR HERBAL TEA ICE CUBES

Green tea ice cubes supply extra antioxidants, while herbal tea ice cubes provide the benefits of the plants they contain.

RECYCLING
LEFTOVERS

How wasteful it would be to throw out all those leftover organic fruits and vegetables you have carefully selected for your detox waters? In order to get the maximum benefit from their health-promoting properties, even if they become a bit paler or less tasty following maceration, you can still make use of their fibre and their non-water-soluble nutrients (see recipes on pages 110–121).

SMOOTHIES FROM SCRAPS

The easiest way of re-using the fruit and vegetable scraps from detox waters is to turn them into a smoothie. Using a blender, process the detox water leftovers, adding fruit juice (preferably homemade), spices and a sweetening ingredient according to taste.

READY-COOKED DELICACIES

How you use the detox water leftovers and what you combine them with depends on their water content. If they are dry and fibrous, they can be folded into a cake or pancake dough. If, on the other hand, they're watery, they will need to be heated or combined with more fibre-rich ingredients.

PAGE 28

PAGE 32

PAGE 4

PAGE 40

18

PAGE 50

DETOX WATERS FOR

Spring & Summer

FINE SUNNY DAYS ARE ESPECIALLY SUITED TO MAKING REFRESHING SWEET-SMELLING DRINKS. CHOOSE SOFT SUMMER BERRIES AND YELLOW-FLESHED FRUITS, BUT PAIR THEM WITH AROMATIC HERBS. IF POSSIBLE, HEAD OUTSIDE AND GATHER YOUR OWN FRUIT.

SUMMER WATER WITH
MELON & STRAWBERRY

PREPARATION TIME **5 MIN**
INFUSION TIME **12 HRS**

150g (5½ oz.) melon flesh

juice of 1 whole lemon

150g (5½ oz.) strawberries
+ 1l (32 fl oz./1 quart) water

NUTRITIONAL **BENEFITS**

MELON
It is the carotenoids in the flesh of a melon that give it its beautiful orange hue. Melon contains carotene, as well as small amounts of lutein and zeaxanthin, which are beneficial for eyesight. Choose melon varieties such as Cantaloupe and Charentais that have deep orange flesh, rather than the paler varieties.

STRAWBERRIES
Rich in flavonoids, as well as containing vitamin C and manganese, strawberries help to protect the body against certain cancers.

1L (32 FL OZ.)

• Chop the melon flesh into small pieces and cut the strawberries in half.
• Place all the ingredients together in a jar.
• Leave to infuse for at least 12 hours in the refrigerator before serving.

WHITE TEA WITH

BLACKBERRY & VANILLA

PREPARATION TIME **5 MIN**
INFUSION TIME **12 HRS**

juice of 1 whole lemon
+ 1l (32 fl oz/1 quart) water

350g (12½ oz.) blackberries

1 vanilla pod

1 tbsp.
white tea leaves

NUTRITIONAL **BENEFITS**

WHITE TEA
All tea comes from the same plant, *camellia sinensis*, but it is the drying and fermentation processes that take place after the leaves are picked that gives them their specific flavour and nutritional qualities. White and green teas are both rich in antioxidants. White tea is made up of only the youngest leaves and buds.

BLACKBERRIES
One of the richest fruits in red antioxidants, the anthocyanidins in blackberries protect the intestinal cells from oxidation.

1L (32 FL OZ.)

• Place the tea leaves in a muslin bag or a ball-shaped tea infuser.
• Split the vanilla bean in half lengthways and scrape out the seeds.
• Place all the ingredients together in a jar.
• Leave to infuse for at least 12 hours in the refrigerator before serving.

21

SUMMER WATER WITH

REDCURRANTS, WATERMELON & MULBERRIES

PREPARATION TIME **5 MIN**
INFUSION TIME **12 HRS**

200g (7 oz.) watermelon flesh

150g (5½ oz.) redcurrants

60g (2 oz.) mulberries
(or raisins)
+ 1l (32 fl oz./1 quart) water

NUTRITIONAL **BENEFITS**

1L (32 FL OZ.)

REDCURRANTS
These small currants are packed with vitamin C, potassium and pectin – a soluble fibre. After drinking the detox water, eat the fruit.

WATERMELON
The antioxidants in watermelon flesh are mainly carotenoids, which play a preventative role in the development of certain cancers and fight inflammation.

MULBERRIES
Rich in iron, calcium and vitamin C, mulberries add a slight sweetness to the detox water.

- Strip the redcurrants from their stalk.
- Chop the watermelon flesh into small pieces.
- Place all the ingredients together in a jar.
- Leave to infuse for at least 12 hours in the refrigerator before serving.

MEADOWSWEET TEA
WITH CUCUMBER

PREPARATION TIME **5 MIN**
INFUSION TIME **12 HRS**

200g (7 oz.) cucumber

1 tsp. dried meadowsweet leaves

Juice of 1 whole lemon
* 1l (32 fl oz./1 quart) water

NUTRITIONAL **BENEFITS**

MEADOWSWEET
The meadowsweet plant can be found growing abundantly in fields during summer and is easy to harvest and dry. It contains salicylic aldehyde, which is found in aspirin. Infusions made with meadowsweet are used primarily as a diuretic and to aid slimming and combat cellulite.

CUCUMBER
When consumed with the skin on, cucumber contains antioxidants, copper and vitamin K.

1L (32 FL OZ.)

• Chop the cucumber into slices.
• Place the dried meadowsweet leaves in a muslin bag or a ball-shaped tea infuser.
• Place all the ingredients together in a jar.
• Leave to infuse for at least 12 hours in the refrigerator before serving.

LAVENDER WATER
WITH BLUEBERRIES

PREPARATION TIME **5 MIN**
INFUSION TIME **12 HRS**

juice of 1 whole lemon
+ 1l (32 fl oz./1 quart) water

1 tbsp. lavender flowers,
dried or fresh

300g (10½ oz.) blueberries

NUTRITIONAL **BENEFITS**

BLUEBERRIES
Higher than that of any other small berry, the blueberry is prized for its high antioxidant content. The flavonoids the blueberry contains are particularly effective in slowing the spread of cancer cells and tumours. Whenever possible, choose wild blueberries over the cultivated varieties.

LAVENDER
This aromatic plant is used for its natural calming, healing and antiseptic properties.

1L (32 FL OZ.)

• Lightly crush the blueberries to burst their skins or, if very large, cut the berries in half.
• Place the lavender flowers in a muslin bag or a ball-shaped tea infuser.
• Place all the ingredients together in a jar.
• Leave to infuse for at least 12 hours in the refrigerator before serving.

A PERFECT MATCH WITH SUMMER FRUITS

Lavender pairs beautifully with most summer fruits: melon, peach, apricots, strawberries, raspberries... Do not hesitate to substitute any of these fruits in place of the blueberries.

COCONUT WATER
WITH CARROT
& BANANA

PREPARATION TIME **5 MIN**
INFUSION TIME **12 HRS**

2 carrots

juice of 1 whole lemon

600ml (20 fl oz./2½ cups) coconut water

2 bananas

coconut milk ice cubes (see page 122), to serve + 300ml (10 fl oz./1¼ cups) water

NUTRITIONAL **BENEFITS**

BANANAS
As well as its high vitamin B6 and manganese content, bananas are reputed to be very alkalizing, helping to maintain the proper functioning of intestinal flora. When bananas are not overly ripe, they contain starch that helps to regulate blood glucose levels.

COCONUT WATER
This hydrating water is the clear liquid from young green coconuts. It is rich in minerals and vitamins from the B group.

1L (32 FL OZ.)

• Chop the carrots and bananas into slices.
• Place the carrot and banana slices into a jar. Add the lemon juice, coconut water and water.
• Leave to infuse for at least 12 hours in the refrigerator before serving.
• Serve with the coconut milk ice cubes.

NETTLE WATER

WITH COCONUT

PREPARATION TIME **5 MIN**
INFUSION TIME **12 HRS**

1 fresh coconut

Juice of 1 whole lemon

+ 900ml (30½ fl oz/4 cups) water

1 tbsp. dried nettle leaves
(or 1 cup fresh nettle leaves)

NUTRITIONAL **BENEFITS**

1L (32 FL OZ.)

NETTLES
Widely considered to be a weed, and found in both gardens and along country roads, nettles are rich in silica, as well as vitamins A and C. Nettle tea infused with the leaves of the plant is recommended to help ease rheumatism.

COCONUTS
The sweet flavour of coconut flesh pairs beautifully with the nettles.

• Break open the coconut, pour out the water and the chop the flesh into small pieces.
• Place the nettle leaves in a muslin bag or a ball-shaped tea infuser.
• Place all the ingredients together in a jar.
• Leave to infuse for at least 12 hours in the refrigerator before serving.

WATERMELON REFRESHER
WITH MINT

PREPARATION TIME **5 MIN**
INFUSION TIME **12 HRS**

400g (14 oz.) watermelon flesh

juice of 1 whole lemon

25 fresh mint leaves
+ 1l (32 fl oz./1 quart)
water

NUTRITIONAL **BENEFITS**

WATERMELON
Just like melon, watermelon flesh contains carotenoids, and in particular lycopene. This fights inflammation and cholesterol. It is also one of the richest foods in citrulline, an amino acid that is beneficial to blood vessels.

MINT
Highly refreshing, mint is very easy to grow either in the garden or in pots on a balcony. Mint contains vitamin K, which plays a key role in blood clotting.

1L (32 FL OZ.)

• Chop the watermelon flesh into chunks.
• Tear the largest mint leaves in half.
• Place all the ingredients together in a jar.
• Leave to infuse for at least 12 hours in the refrigerator before serving.

For an intensely
aromatic detox
water, use the
sweetest, ripest
watermelon you
can find.

VANILLA WATER
WITH PLUMS

PREPARATION TIME **5 MIN**
INFUSION TIME **12 HRS**

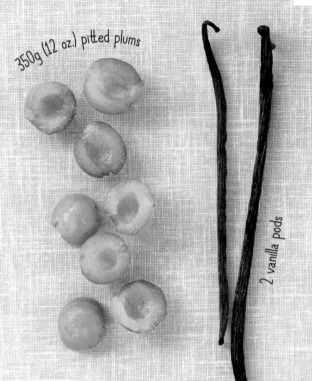

350g (12 oz.) pitted plums

2 vanilla pods

juice of 1 whole lemon
+ 1l (32 fl oz./1 quart) water

NUTRITIONAL **BENEFITS**

1L (32 FL OZ.)

PLUMS

The antioxidants present in plums are mainly flavonoids, as well as phenolic acid. Regular consumption of plums can help to lower bad cholesterol. Some recent studies conducted on animals showed a favourable reaction to anxiety levels when fed plums. Plums also contain a small amount of iron and vitamin B6. As an alternative to plums, try this recipe using nectarines.

• Chop the pitted plums in half.
• Split the vanilla beans in half lengthways and scrape out the seeds.
• Place all the ingredients together in a jar.
• Leave to infuse for at least 12 hours in the refrigerator before serving.

COCONUT WATER
WITH MATCHA TEA
& RASPBERRIES

PREPARATION TIME **5 MIN**
INFUSION TIME **12 HRS**

200g (7 oz.) raspberries

600ml (20 fl oz./2½ cups) coconut water
+ 400ml (14 fl oz./1¾ cups) water

½ tsp. matcha tea powder

juice of 1 whole lemon

NUTRITIONAL **BENEFITS**

1L (32 FL OZ.)

COCONUT WATER
You can harvest the coconut water from a fresh coconut or buy a carton. Either way, you will benefit from its rich intensity of vitamins and minerals.

MATCHA TEA
This Japanese green tea, reduced to a fine powder, is rich in calcium and antioxidants. A little bitter in taste, it works well paired with acidic flavours, such as raspberry and lemon juice. Additionally, the vitamin C in lemon juice helps to preserve the antioxidants.

• Mix the matcha tea powder with a little water.
• Place all the ingredients together in a jar.
• Leave to infuse for at least 12 hours in the refrigerator before serving.
• If preferred, serve with coconut milk ice cubes (see page 122).

SUMMER WATER WITH

TOMATOES, RASPBERRIES & BASIL

PREPARATION TIME **5 MIN**
INFUSION TIME **12 HRS**

juice of 1 whole lemon

8 basil leaves

125g (4½ oz.) cherry tomatoes

250g (9 oz.) raspberries
+ 1l (32 fl oz./1 quart) water

NUTRITIONAL **BENEFITS**

TOMATOES & RASPBERRIES
Lycopene gives tomatoes their attractive red colour, whilst it is the anthocyanins in raspberries that tint the fruit pink. In both cases, these powerful antioxidants help to prevent the development of cancers and cardiovascular disease.

BASIL
Fresh basil leaves are a good source of vitamin K and contain a small amount of iron.

1L (32 FL OZ.)

• Chop the cherry tomatoes in half.
• Tear any larger basil leaves into smaller pieces.
• Place all the ingredients together in a jar.
• Leave to infuse for at least 12 hours in the refrigerator before serving.

SUMMER
FRUITS

Basil successfully takes on the flavour of raspberries and, in general, any other red soft fruit. As a summery alternative, replace the raspberries with ripe strawberries.

ROSEMARY WATER

FOR REHYDRATION

PREPARATION TIME **5 MIN**
INFUSION TIME **12 HRS**

1 sprig of rosemary

× *Juice of ½ lemon*
200ml (6¾ fl oz.) water

NUTRITIONAL **BENEFITS**

LEMON & ROSEMARY
Both these ingredients enhance the detoxifying function of the liver. Prepare this detox water the day before in order to have a rich infusion of active ingredients ready to drink in the morning. Overnight our bodies lose water and often we awake dehydrated. Drink a large glass of this infusion on waking to rehydrate the body, which will also benefit from the alkalizing and cleansing effects of the lemon.

1 GLASS

• The prevous night, fill a glass with water and immerse a spring of rosemary in the glass.
• Leave to infuse overnight in the refrigerator.
• Before serving, squeeze the juice of half a lemon into the glass.
NOTE
Add a drop of birch sap, noted for its detoxifying and purifying properties.

FRUIT WATER WITH

RED BELL PEPPER,
BANANA & STRAWBERRIES

PREPARATION TIME **5 MIN**
INFUSION TIME **12 HRS**

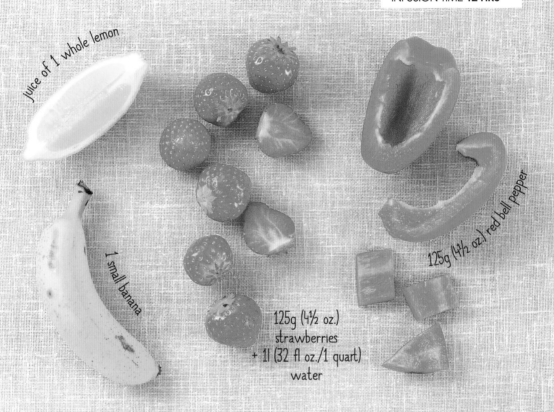

Juice of 1 whole lemon

1 small banana

125g (4½ oz.)
strawberries
+ 1l (32 fl oz./1 quart)
water

125g (4½ oz.) red bell pepper

NUTRITIONAL **BENEFITS**

BANANAS
Although bananas are not often grouped with fruits that contain the most antioxidants, such as strawberries, they do contain dopamine, which is a powerful antioxdant.

RED BELL PEPPERS
A red bell pepper is simply a ripe green bell pepper. When eaten raw, they are a great source of vitamins A, C and B6, along with pantothenic acid (vitamin B5).

1L (32 FL OZ.)

• Chop the banana into slices.
• Chop the strawberries into halves or quarters, depending on their size.
• Chop the red bell pepper into small pieces.
• Place all the ingredients together in a jar.
• Leave to infuse for at least 12 hours in the refrigerator before serving.

SUNSHINE WATER

WITH YELLOW SUMMER FRUITS

PREPARATION TIME **5 MIN**
INFUSION TIME **12 HRS**

1 peach

150g (5½ oz.) melon flesh

4 apricots
+ 1l (32 fl oz./1 quart) water
+ coconut milk or almond milk ice cubes
(see page 122), to serve

NUTRITIONAL **BENEFITS**

YELLOW FRUITS

All the yellow summer fruits contain a high concentration of carotenoids (beta-carotene, zeaxanthin and lutein). These antioxidants are water-soluble and are especially beneficial to eyesight. To maximize the absorption of these antioxidants, accompany this detox water with coconut milk or almond milk ice cubes. The leftover fruits from the detox water can be eaten — accompany them with a handful of almonds for a healthy fat.

1L (32 FL OZ.)

- Cut the apricots and peach into halves, then remove the stones.
- Chop all the fruit into small pieces.
- Place all the ingredients together in a jar.
- Leave to infuse for at least 12 hours in the refrigerator before serving.
- Serve with the coconut milk or almond milk ice cubes.

EAT THE MACERATED FRUIT
FOR MAXIMUM BENEFIT

To get the maximum benefit from the beta-carotene, eat the macerated fruit as well as drinking the detox water and the ice cubes.

LEMON BALM WATER

WITH FENNEL SEEDS

PREPARATION TIME **5 MIN**
INFUSION TIME **12 HRS**

1 tsp. fennel seeds

juice of 1 whole lemon
+ 1L (32 fl oz./1 quart) water

20g (¾ oz.) fresh lemon balm leaves

NUTRITIONAL **BENEFITS**

LEMON BALM AND FENNEL SEEDS

In herbal medicine both lemon balm and fennel seeds are traditionally known to relieve stomach ailments and stimulate digestion. Lemon balm can also be recommended for nausea and dizziness, and fennel seeds are a good general health tonic.

1L (32 FL OZ.)

• Crush the fennel seeds with a pestle and mortar.
• Tear the largest lemon balm leaves.
• Place all the ingredients together in a jar.
• Leave to infuse for at least 12 hours in the refrigerator before serving.

GREEN TEA
WITH MINT & BASIL

PREPARATION TIME **5 MIN**
INFUSION TIME **12 HRS**

juice of 1 whole lemon

20 mint leaves

1 tbsp. green tea

20 basil leaves

1 (32 fl oz./1 quart) water

NUTRITIONAL **BENEFITS**

GREEN TEA
A star amongst health drinks, green tea has antioxidant and diuretic properties. However, like all teas, it prevents the proper absorption of iron so it is best consumed other than at mealtimes.

MINT AND BASIL
Like all fresh herbs, mint and basil contain a healthy supply of antioxidants, which help to prevent many age-related diseases.

1L (32 FL OZ.)

• Place the green tea in a muslin bag or a ball-shaped tea infuser.
• Place all the ingredients together in a jar.
• Leave to infuse for at least 12 hours in the refrigerator before serving.

RUBY WATER
WITH MIXED RED FRUITS &
HIBISCUS FLOWERS

PREPARATION TIME **5 MIN**
INFUSION TIME **12 HRS**

juice of 1 whole lemon

2 tbsp.
dried hibiscus flowers
* 1l (32 fl oz./1 quart) water

250g (9 oz.) mixed red fruits
(cherries, strawberries, raspberries...)

NUTRITIONAL **BENEFITS**

1L (32 FL OZ.)

RED FRUITS
Rich in antioxidants and vitamin C, they are believed to be a great help in preventing the onset of certain cancers.

HIBISCUS
Tea brewed with hibiscus is popular across North Africa, especially in Egypt, where it is known as karkadé. Rich in vitamin C, which gives the drink its tart flavour, hibiscus flowers contain anthocyanins that are beneficial for patients with mild hypertension.

- Place all the ingredients together in a jar.
- Leave to infuse for at least 12 hours in the refrigerator before serving.

EDIBLE FLOWERS

MAKE AN
ORIGINAL DESSERT

Do not throw away the red fruits or hibiscus flowers! Enjoy them with a little cottage cheese and granola or try the smoothie recipe on page 110.

REFRESHING WATER

WITH LEMONGRASS & VERBENA

PREPARATION TIME **5 MIN**
INFUSION TIME **12 HRS**

4 sticks of lemongrass

1 tbsp. dried lemon verbena

juice of 1 whole lemon
+ 1l (32 fl oz./1 quart) water

NUTRITIONAL **BENEFITS**

LEMON VERBENA
Like all fresh herbs, verbena is very rich in antioxidants. It is a natural diuretic and is recommended in cases of stomach pain, headaches and spasms.

LEMONGRASS
Useful for its antiseptic properties, the light scent of verbena combines wonderfully with lemongrass.

LEMON
Adding lemon juice to the detox water boosts the antioxidant and vitamin C levels.

1L (32 FL OZ.)

• Place the lemon verbena in a muslin bag or a ball-shaped tea infuser.
• Cut the lemongrass into quarters lengthways, then in half again.
• Place all the ingredients together in a jar.
• Leave to infuse for at least 12 hours in the refrigerator before serving.

TONIC WATER WITH

STRAWBERRY & RHUBARB

PREPARATION TIME **5 MIN**
INFUSION TIME **12 HRS**

250g (9 oz.) strawberries

Juice of 1 whole lime
+ 1l (32 fl oz./1 quart) water

150g (5½ oz.) rhubarb

NUTRITIONAL **BENEFITS**

STRAWBERRIES
When eaten regularly, strawberries help the body to combat certain cancers and chronic diseases. They also have anti-inflammatory properties.

RHUBARB
Rhubard is especially rich in vitamin K, although its antioxidant content will be partly degraded during the cooking process. Make the most of the fibre in the fruit by using the leftover fruit from the detox water to make a delicious chutney (see page 120).

1L (32 FL OZ.)

• Chop the rhubarb into pieces.
• Chop the strawberries into small pieces.
• Place all the ingredients together in a jar.
• Leave to infuse for at least 12 hours in the refrigerator before serving.

SUMMER WATER

WITH PEACH, COURGETTE & THYME

PREPARATION TIME 5 MIN
INFUSION TIME 12 HRS

4 sprigs of rosemary

2 peaches

70g (2½ oz.) courgette
(zucchini)
+ juice of 1 whole lemon
+ 1l (32 fl oz./1 quart) water

NUTRITIONAL **BENEFITS**

1L (32 FL OZ.)

PEACH & COURGETTE
Both contain phenolic compounds to fight against low-density lipoprotein cholesterol, thereby protecting against cardiovascular disease. Both are rich in carotenoids, including lutein, an antioxidant that is beneficial for eyesight.

ROSEMARY
In traditional herbal medicine, rosemary aids the function of the liver and is considered a good general tonic.

- Chop the courgette into slices.
- Cut the peaches in half, remove the stone and then cut each half lengthways into four small pieces.
- Place all the ingredients together in a jar.
- Leave to infuse for at least 12 hours in the refrigerator before serving.

PURIFYING WATER

WITH BIRCH SAP, ROSEMARY & LEMON

PREPARATION TIME **5 MIN**
INFUSION TIME **12 HRS**

8 sprigs of rosemary

2 lemons

400ml (14 fl oz.) birch sap
+ 600ml (21 fl oz.) water

NUTRITIONAL **BENEFITS**

1L (32 FL OZ.)

BIRCH SAP
Best consumed in season during early spring, birch sap is highly purifying and assists the body in eliminating toxins. It can be bought from health food shops.

ROSEMARY & LEMON
Rosemary aids digestion and stimulates the production of bile. Lemon is rich in vitamin C and also acts as a tonic for the liver.

• Peel the lemons and remove all the pith. Cut the lemons into slices.
• Place the rosemary and lemon slices in a jar, then cover with water.
• Leave to infuse for at least 12 hours in the refrigerator before serving.
• Add the birch sap. Serve immediately.

REFRESHING WATER

WITH CUCUMBER, MINT & LEMON

PREPARATION TIME **5 MIN**
INFUSION TIME **12 HRS**

150g (5½ oz.) cucumber

2 small lemons

20 mint leaves
+ 1l (32 fl oz./1 quart) water

NUTRITIONAL **BENEFITS**

CUCUMBER
Consisting of more than 90% water, cucumber is refreshing, hydrating and low in calories. In order to retain the vitamins that it does contain, do not peel a cucumber.

MINT
Idea for combatting a summer heatwave, mint makes a refreshing drink.

LEMON
Lemons are the detox ingredient par excellence. As well as being kind to the liver, lemon is alkalizing and rich in vitamin C.

1L (32 FL OZ.)

• Peel the lemons and remove all the pith, reserving a small strip of lemon peel. Cut the lemons into slices.
• Cut the cucumber into slices.
• Place all the ingredients together in a jar.
• Leave to infuse for at least 12 hours in the refrigerator before serving.

SPARKLING WATER

FOR A FUN
FIZZY DRINK

For a cool fizzy drink, macerate the ingredients in 500ml (17 fl oz.) spring water and then add 500ml (17 fl oz.) of very bubbly water just before serving.

MIXED BERRIES WATER
WITH BASIL

PREPARATION TIME **5 MIN**
INFUSION TIME **12 HRS**

300g (10½ oz.) fresh mixed berries (strawberries, blueberries, raspberries...)

juice of 1 whole lemon

20 basil leaves + 1l (32 fl oz./1 quart) water

NUTRITIONAL **BENEFITS**

1L (32 FL OZ.)

RED FRUITS
Particularly rich in antioxidants, red berries help to prevent ageing and the oxidization of cells. Like all fruits and vegetables, berries contain the most nutrients when freshly picked. Whenever possible, buy locally or pick your own fruit.

BASIL
This herb goes well with red fruits and contains rosmarinic acid, an antioxidant whose effect is enhanced when combined with vitamin E (found in nuts and seeds).

• Cut the strawberries into halves or quarters, depending on their size.
• Lightly crush the blueberries to burst their skins or, if very large, cut the berries in half.
• Tear the larger basil leaves into smaller pieces.
• Place all the ingredients together in a jar.
• Leave to infuse for at least 12 hours in the refrigerator before serving.

FLORAL WATER

WITH CHERRIES
& ROSE PETALS

PREPARATION TIME **5 MIN**
INFUSION TIME **12 HRS**

juice of 1 whole lemon

1 tbsp. dried rose petals
+ 1l (32 fl oz./1 quart) water

350g (12½ oz.) pitted cherries

NUTRITIONAL **BENEFITS**

ROSE
Renowned for its cosmetic qualities, rose can also be used to soothe sore throats. It is indeed a powerful antiseptic.

CHERRIES
Well known for their diuretic properties, cherries are rich in anthocyanins, part of the antioxidant family. These antioxdiants are found especially in acidic varieties of cherries that have ripened in the sun. Therefore avoid cherries out of season when they are ripened artificially.

1L (32 FL OZ.)

• Place the rose petals in a muslin bag or a ball-shaped tea infuser.
• Place all the ingredients together in a jar.
• Leave to infuse for at least 12 hours in the refrigerator before serving.

LEMON WATER

WITH KLAMATH ALGAE

PREPARATION TIME **5 MIN**
INFUSION TIME **12 HRS**

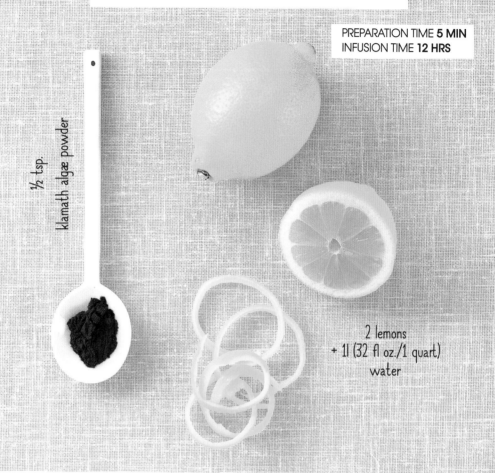

½ tsp.
klamath algæ powder

2 lemons
+ 1l (32 fl oz./1 quart)
water

NUTRITIONAL **BENEFITS**

KLAMATH ALGAE

Sold in powdered form as a food supplement, klamath algae disperses instantly in water and colours it a beautiful bright blue. This powerful algae reduces fatigue and boosts mental ability. Harvested only in one place in the world, this microalgae is taken from surface of the Klamath lake in the United States. But be sure to by a brand that is certified organic, which will ensure there are no contaminants in the product.

1L (32 FL OZ.)

• Peel the lemons and remove all the pith, reserving a small strip of lemon peel. Cut the lemons into slices.
• Place all the ingredients together in a jar, then quickly stir to dissolve the powdered algae.
• Leave to infuse for at least 12 hours in the refrigerator before serving.

USE POWDERED ALGAE

ONLY FROM THE
KLAMATH LAKE

Klamath is the only algae that dissolves completely in water. For this reason, do not replace Klamath with Spirulina or Chlorella powder as you will be left with some unappetizing lumps of powder.

REFRESHING WATER

WITH MELON, MINT & BLUEBERRIES

PREPARATION TIME **5 MIN**
INFUSION TIME **12 HRS**

300g (10½ oz.) melon flesh

blueberry ice cubes (see page 122), to serve

20 mint leaves
+ 1l (32 fl oz./1 quart) water

juice of 1 whole lemon

NUTRITIONAL **BENEFITS**

MELON
The antioxidants in melon flesh (lutein and beta-carotene) are not soluble in water, so make sure that you eat the leftover fruit.
MINT
Traditionally used for its digestive properties, mint combats intestinal sluggishness and stimulates the gallbladder.
BLUEBERRIES
Particularly rich in antioxidants from the flavonoid family, blueberries help to combat certain cancers.

1L (32 FL OZ.)

• Cut the melon flesh into small pieces.
• Place all the ingredients together in a jar.
• Leave to infuse for at least 12 hours in the refrigerator before serving..
• Add the blueberry ice cubes and serve immediately.
NOTE
Tear any of the larger mint leaves in half in order to release their fragrant oils.

SPARKLING WHITE TEA
WITH ACEROLA

PREPARATION TIME **5 MIN**
INFUSION TIME **12 HRS**

1 tbsp. acerola powder

1 tbsp. white tea
+ 400ml (14 fl oz.) spring water
+ 600ml (20 fl oz.) sparkling water

NUTRITIONAL **BENEFITS**

WHITE TEA
The antioxidants in white tea are even more abundant than those in green tea. They are effective in lowering cholesterol, blood pressure and cardiovascular disease.

ACEROLA
This little sour cherry preserves the properties of white tea with the antioxidant action of vitamin C, which is exceptionally rich with more than 1,000mg per 100g.

1L (32 FL OZ.)

• Place the white tea in a muslin bag or a ball-shaped tea infuser.
• Dissolve the powdered acerola in a small amount of water, whisking to get rid of lumps.
• Place the tea, acerola and spring water together in a jar.
• Leave to infuse for at least 12 hours in the refrigerator before serving.
• Top up with sparkling water, then serve immediately.

APRICOT WATER
WITH LAVENDER

PREPARATION TIME **5 MIN**
INFUSION TIME **12 HRS**

350g (12 oz.) apricots

4 sprigs of lavender,
fresh or dried

Juice of 1 whole lemon

1l (32 fl oz./1 quart) water

NUTRITIONAL **BENEFITS**

APRICOTS
Choose ripe apricots for their sweet taste and delicious flavour. Rich in vitamin A, iron and copper, be sure to eat the leftover fruit to gain maximum benfiefit – ideally consume with a healthy fat, such as a handful of almonds.

LAVENDER
This potent herb is used for its relaxing effects. In the form of an essential oil, it also helps to relieve migraines when mixed with a little neutral oil and used to massage the temples.

1L (32 FL OZ.)

• Cut the apricots in half and remove the stones. Cut each apricot half into three or four small pieces.
• Place all the ingredients together in a jar.
• Leave to infuse for at least 12 hours in the refrigerator before serving.

VITAMIN WATER

WITH DRIED APRICOT

& RHUBARB

PREPARATION TIME **5 MIN**
INFUSION TIME **12 HRS**

10 dried apricots

400g (14 oz.) rhubarb

juice of 1 whole lemon
+ 1l (32 fl oz./1 quart) water

NUTRITIONAL **BENEFITS**

RHUBARB
It is rich in vitamins K and C, calcium and manganese. Feel free to cook the leftover fruit to make a compote in order to to benefifit from their fibre content.

DRIED APRICOTS
More concentrated than fresh fruit, dried apricots are rich in vitamins and many minerals, including iron, copper, magnesium, phosphorus, and potassium. After drinking the detox water, eat the leftover fruit with yoghurt, muesli or use it to make a compote.

1L (32 FL OZ.)

• Cut the apricots into small pieces.
• Cut the rhubarb into chunks.
• Place all the ingredients together in a jar.
• Leave to infuse for at least 12 hours in the refrigerator before serving.

55

GARDEN HERB WATER
WITH LEMON

PREPARATION TIME **5 MIN**
INFUSION TIME **12 HRS**

15g (½ oz.) parsley
+ 1l (32 fl oz./1 quart) water

5g (¼ oz.) tarragon

juice of 1 whole lemon

15g (½ oz.) coriander

10g (⅓ oz.) sage

NUTRITIONAL **BENEFITS**

1L (32 FL OZ.)

FRESH GARDEN HERBS
Garden have a very interesting antioxidant power, fighting against the harmful free radicals in the body and helping to prevent aging. Furthermore, they are source of vitamin K and iron. Sage is also beneficial to the proper functioning of the liver, and tarragon helps to relieve anxiety disorders. For this recipe, only the uppermost part of the stems is used.

• Place all the ingredients together in a jar.
• Leave to infuse for at least 12 hours in the refrigerator before serving.

DON'T THROW IT AWAY

MAKE AN
EXTRAORDINARY PESTO

Recycle the leftover
herbs from this
detox water
infusion by making
the pesto recipe
on page 123.

REFRESHING WATER
WITH PEACH, VANILLA & ALMOND

PREPARATION TIME **5 MIN**
INFUSION TIME **12 HRS**

3 peaches

almond milk ice cubes (see page 122), to serve

1 vanilla pod
+ juice of 1 whole lemon
+ 1l (32 fl oz./1 quart)
water

NUTRITIONAL **BENEFITS**

PEACH
The antioxidants in peaches are contained mainly in their skins, so it is imperative to choose organic peaches that do not need peeling. To harness all of the nutrients in the peaches, as they are not entirely water soluable, eat the leftover fruit along with the detox water and ice cubes.

VANILLA
Useful for its properties that can help to combat stress, fatigue and insomnia. Reuse the vanilla pod in a smoothie, for example.

1L (32 FL OZ.)

• Cut the peaches in half, remove the stones and cut into strips. Split the vanilla pod in half lengthwise and chop into two or three pieces.
• Place the peach and the vanilla together in a jar. Add the lemon juice and the water.
• Leave to infuse for at least 12 hours in the refrigerator before serving.
• Serve with almond milk ice cubes.

INFUSION

WITH DETOXIFYING HERBS

PREPARATION TIME **5 MIN**
INFUSION TIME **12 HRS**

10g (⅓ oz.) cherry stalks

1 tbsp. red vine

juice of 1 whole lemon

1 tbsp. meadowsweet

1 tbsp. orthosiphon (or green tea) +
1l (32 fl oz./1 quart) water

NUTRITIONAL **BENEFITS**

This infusion will help to figh cellulite when drunk during the day, but not at mealtimes.
CHERRY STALKS
It is used for its diuretic properties. Feel free to use the tails of wild cherries picked yourself.
MEADOWSWEET, ORTHOSIPHON AND RED VINE
Meadowsweet and orthosiphon fight water retention. Red vine helps to detoxify the body while promoting circulation.

1L (32 FL OZ.)

• Put the herbal ingredients into a muslin bag or ball-shaped tea infuser.
• Place all the ingredients together in a jar.
• Leave to infuse for at least 12 hours in the refrigerator before serving.

LIME WATER
WITH ANISEED

PREPARATION TIME **5 MIN**
INFUSION TIME **12 HRS**

3 tbsp. dried lime leaves

juice of 1 whole lemon
+ 1 (32 fl oz./1 quart) water

1 tsp. green aniseed seeds

NUTRITIONAL **BENEFITS**

LIME LEAVES
Traditionally taken as an infusion in the evening, lime leaves can aid sleep, relieve stress and quell anxiety. In herbal medicine, it can also be used for its draining properties, in the case of kidney stones in particular.

GREEN ANISEED
An antispasmodic that helps soothe aching stomachs, green aniseed also fights against nervous disorders.

1L (32 FL OZ.)

• Grind the aniseed with a pestle and mortar.
• Place all the ingredients together in a jar.
• Leave to infuse for at least 12 hours in the refrigerator before serving.

CITRUS WATER

WITH ORANGE BLOSSOMS

PREPARATION TIME **5 MIN**
INFUSION TIME **12 HRS**

2 oranges

1 tsp. orange blossoms

juice of 1 whole lemon
+ 1l (32 fl oz./1 quart) water

NUTRITIONAL **BENEFITS**

ORANGES
Rich in vitamin C and various antioxidants from the carotenoid family, oranges are also high in calcium, copper and vitamin B. Recent studies also indicate that hesperetin, a key antioxidant found in oranges, decreases the risk of cerebrovascular disease.

ORANGE BLOSSOMS
Often used as a flavouring in baking, orange blossoms have calming properties.

1L (32 FL OZ.)

• Place the orange blossoms in a muslin bag or a ball-shaped tea infuser.
• Take a thin strip of peel from one of the oranges. Peel the oranges and remove the pith, then cut the flesh into slices.
• Place all the ingredients together in a jar.
• Leave to infuse for at least 12 hours in the refrigerator before serving.

PAGE 66

PAGE 70

PAGE 9

PAGE 78

PAGE 102

DETOX WATERS FOR

Autumn & Winter

AS THE SEASONS TURN COLDER, FRUIT BECOMES SCARCER, SO STOCK UP ON VITAMIN-C WITH CITRUS-RICH DETOX WATERS. AUTUMN AND WINTER ARE ALSO GOOD TIMES OF THE YEAR TO PAMPER YOURSELF WITH HEALTH-ENHANCING PLANT INFUSIONS AND HERBAL TEAS.

ANTIOXIDANT WATER
WITH POMEGRANATE
& BANANA

PREPARATION TIME **5 MIN**
INFUSION TIME **12 HRS**

1 pomegranate

2 bananas

juice of 1 whole lemon + 1l (32 fl oz./1 quart) water

NUTRITIONAL **BENEFITS**

1L (32 FL OZ.)

POMEGRANATE
This is one of the most beneficial fruit for its antioxidant content, which is more active than that of green tea and red grapes. Anthocyanins are what give pomegranate seeds their red colour. Pomegranate is believed to prevent some cancers, cardiovascular disease and certain neurological disorders.

BANANA
Besides being alkalizing and beneficial for intestinal flora, bananas are also believed to play a role in preventing certain cancers.

• Cut the bananas into slices.
• Chop the pomegranate in half and remove the seeds, discarding the white skins.
• Gently crush the pomegranate seeds.
• Place all the ingredients together in a jar.
• Leave to infuse for at least 12 hours in the refrigerator before serving.

PURIFYING WATER
WITH BLACK RADISH
& PEPPERMINT

PREPARATION TIME **5 MIN**
INFUSION TIME **12 HRS**

1 tsp. dried peppermint

250g (9 oz.) black radish

Juice of 1 whole lemon
+ 1l (32 fl oz./1 quart) water

NUTRITIONAL **BENEFITS**

BLACK RADISH
An edible root vegetable, the black radish is part of the same family as the turnip. It is traditionally used for its purifying properties and its postive effect on the liver function, but it is also believed to protect against some cancers and age-related memory loss.

PEPPERMINT
Peppermint is reputed to calm any irritated intestines and stimulate digestion.

1L (32 FL OZ.)

• Rinse and wipe the black radish, then cut into thin strips.
• Place the dried peppermint in a tea ball.
• Place all the ingredients together in a jar.
• Leave to infuse for at least 12 hours in the refrigerator before serving.

SPARKLING KIWI COCKTAIL

WITH PINEAPPLE

PREPARATION TIME **5 MIN**
INFUSION TIME **12 HRS**

200g (7 oz.) pineapple flesh

2 kiwi fruits

juice of 1 whole lemon
+ 500ml (17 fl oz.) spring water
+ 500ml (17 fl oz.) sparkling water

NUTRITIONAL **BENEFITS**

PINEAPPLE
The enzyme, bromelain, contained in pineapples has multiple beneficial properties: it is an anti-inflammatory, helps to prevent tumors, and is beneficial to the digestion and blood. Pineapples are also rich in manganese.

KIWI
Kiwi fruits are an important source of vitamin K, and one of the fruits richest in vitamin C, which is a powerful antioxidant.

1L (32 FL OZ.)

• Chop the pineapple flesh into pieces.
• Peel the kiwi fruits and cut them into pieces.
• Place the chopped fruit with the lemon juice and spring water in a jar.
• Leave to infuse for at least 12 hours in the refrigerator before serving.
• When ready to serve, add the sparkling water to the drink.

TO ENHANCE THE
FRUIT FLAVOURS

Add a few sprigs of
fresh coriander
(cilantro); its fresh
herb fragrance
blends well with
pineapple.

67

AUTUMNAL WATER

WITH APPLE, PEAR
& WARMING SPICES

1 pear

1 apple

5cm (2 in.) fresh ginger

6 cloves + 1 tsp. black peppercorns
+ 1l (32 fl oz./1 quart) water

4 sticks of cinnamon

NUTRITIONAL **BENEFITS**

1L (32 FL OZ.)

APPLE
Considered an everyday fruit, apples are often overlooked. As with all fruits, apples contain a lot of antioxidants, vitamins and fibre. In addition, apples reduce the risk of cardiovascular disease and help to lower bad cholesterol.

PEAR
Pears are a rich source of antioxidants and fibre, which lie mainly in the skin of the fruit. Because of this, it is import not to peel pears and choose organic fruit whenever possible.

• Remove the stalk and core of the apple and pear and cut them into slices.
• Peel the ginger and slice it into thin strips.
• Crush the cinnamon sticks, cloves and peppercorns with a pestle and mortar, then place them in a muslin bag or ball-shaped tea infuser.
• Place all the ingredients together in a jar.
• Leave to infuse for at least 12 hours in the refrigerator before serving.

APPETIZING WATER

WITH MANGO

& TURMERIC

PREPARATION TIME **5 MIN**
INFUSION TIME **12 HRS**

350g (12 oz.) mango flesh

15g (½ oz.) fresh turmeric
(3 pieces)

juice of 1 whole lemon
+ 1l (32 fl oz./1 quart) water

NUTRITIONAL **BENEFITS**

1L (32 FL OZ.)

MANGO
Antioxidant-rich with polyphenols and carotenoids, mango helps to protect cells from the oxidation caused by free radicals. The fruit also contains vitamin C and E, plus B vitamins.

TURMERIC
Turmeric has anti-inflammatory properties that have a beneficial effect on gastro-intestinal system. Turmeric is rich in curcumin, an antioxidant whose effect is optimized when it is eaten with pepper.

- Peel the turmeric and cut it into thin slices.
- Chop the mango into small pieces.
- Place all the ingredients together in a jar.
- Leave to infuse for at least 12 hours in the refrigerator before serving.

CARROT CAKE
IN A DRINK

PREPARATION TIME **5 MIN**
INFUSION TIME **12 HRS**

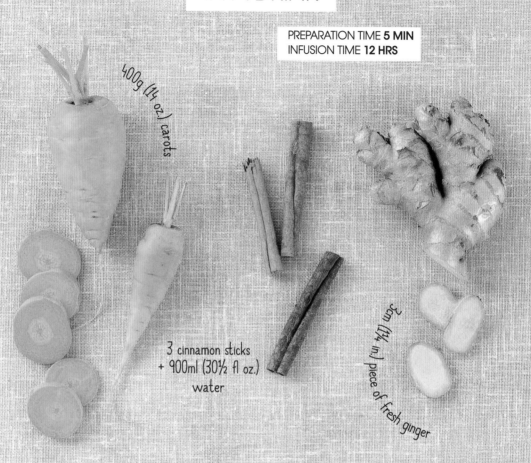

400g (14 oz.) carrots

3 cinnamon sticks
+ 900ml (30½ fl oz.)
water

3cm (1¼ in.) piece of fresh ginger

NUTRITIONAL **BENEFITS**

1L (32 FL OZ.)

CARROT
As the name suggests, carrots are a good source of carotenoids, including lutein and zeaxanthin, antioxidants that are beneficial for eyesight. Like all carotenoids, they are not water-soluble but rather fat-soluble, so they therefore need to be eaten with a source of healthy fat in order to be assimilated properly. Carrots are also a source of vitamins K, C and E, as well as B vitamins, iron, phosphorus and potassium.

• Cut the carrots into slices.
• Slice the ginger into thin strips.
• Break the cinnamon sticks into two or three pieces or crush them with a pestle and mortar. Place them in a muslin bag.
• Place all the ingredients together in a jar.
• Leave to infuse for at least 12 hours in the refrigerator before serving. Serve with almond milk ice cubes, if preferred (see page 122).
NOTE
Use the leftover residue of this recipe by making the pancakes (see page 118).

If you can find them
at your local
farmers' market,
use purple carrots
rather than orange
ones. They are rich
in antioxidants.

PEAR WATER
WITH FENNEL & GINGER

PREPARATION TIME **5 MIN**
INFUSION TIME **12 HRS**

2 small pears

125g (5½ oz.) fennel bulb

juice of 1 whole lemon
+ 6cm (2½ in.) fresh ginger
+ 1l (32 fl oz./1 quart) water

NUTRITIONAL **BENEFITS**

PEAR
Rich in antioxidants from the family of phenolic compounds, such as flavonoids, pears play a preventive role in the development of certain cancers. The pear is also a good source of fibre, mainly present in the skin, which helps to regulate intestinal transit.

FENNEL & GINGER
Both fennel and ginger have a positive effect on the digestive system. Fennel is also a source of vitamin C , while ginger is rich in copper and manganese.

1L (32 FL OZ.)

• Chop the pears into quarters and remove the cores. Chop each pear quarter in small chunks or thin slices.
• Chop the fennel into small pieces.
• Slice the ginger thinly.
• Place all the ingredients together in a jar.
• Leave to infuse for at least 12 hours in the refrigerator before serving.

NOTE
Make the green smoothie recipe (see page 112) using the residue of this detox water in order to reap the benefits of the pear fibre.

ROOIBOS INFUSION

WITH LIQUORICE

PREPARATION TIME **5 MIN**
INFUSION TIME **12 HRS**

1½ tbsp.
rooibos (or 2 teabags)
+ 1l (32 fl oz./1 quart) water

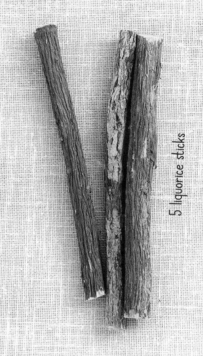

5 liquorice sticks

NUTRITIONAL **BENEFITS**

ROOIBOS
Despite its name of 'red tea', rooibos is actually the bark of a South African tree that is fermented, then dried and drunk as a tea. It contains no caffeine, but does contain some polyphenols, including Aspalathin, of which it is the only known source.

LIQUORICE
Liquorice has a positive effect on stomach ulcers. However, it is not recommended for pregnant women or people with hypertension.

1L (32 FL OZ.)

• Place the rooibos in a muslin bag or ball-shaped tea infuser.
• Place all the ingredients together in a jar.
• Leave to infuse for at least 12 hours in the refrigerator before serving.

GREEN TEA
WITH CITRUS

PREPARATION TIME **5 MIN**
INFUSION TIME **12 HRS**

1 tbsp. green tea

1 lemon
+ 1l (32 fl
oz./1 quart)
water

2 oranges

NUTRITIONAL **BENEFITS**

GREEN TEA
This tea contains antioxidants from the polyphenol family, mainly catechins, theaflavins and thearubigins. With double the antioxidants of black tea, Japanese and Chinese green teas are rich in catechins.

CITRUS
The vitamin C contained in citrus fruits allows the antioxidants present in green tea to be better assimilation.

1L (32 FL OZ.)

• Place the tea in a muslin bag or ball-shaped tea infuser.
• Peel the oranges and lemon and remove all the pith. Cut the fruits into slices.
• Set aside a small strip of both orange peel and lemon rind.
• Place all the ingredients together in a jar.
• Leave to infuse for at least 12 hours in the refrigerator before serving.

ADD A TOUCH
OF SWEETNESS

If you find this
detox water too
bitter, do not
hesitate to add a
little honey
to the infusion.

AUTUMNAL WATER

WITH FIG, CINNAMON
& LEMON

PREPARATION TIME **5 MIN**
INFUSION TIME **12 HRS**

2 fresh figs

4 cinnamon sticks

½ lemon
+ 1l (32 fl oz./1 quart) water

2 dried figs

NUTRITIONAL **BENEFITS**

FIGS
Fresh figs are richer in antioxidants than dried figs, especially if they are dark in colour. They also contain a small amount of carotenoids. Dried figs are rich in minerals, especially calcium, iron and potassium.

CINNAMON
Cinnamon contains a high amount of cinnamaldehyde, an antioxidant with anti-inflammatory and anti-allergic properties.

1L (32 FL OZ.)

• Cut the figs into slices.
• Peel the zest from the lemon. Now squeeze the lemon to extract the juice.
• Break the cinnamon stitcks into two or three pieces or coarsely crush them with a pestle and mortar. Place in a muslin bag.
• Place all the ingredients together in a jar.
• Leave to infuse for at least 12 hours in the refrigerator before serving.

CHICORY WATER

WITH DRIED FRUITS

PREPARATION TIME **5 MIN**
INFUSION TIME **12 HRS**

80g (3 oz.) dates

75g (2¾ oz.) dried apricots

2 tsp. soluble chicory
+ 1l (32 fl oz./1 quart)
water

NUTRITIONAL **BENEFITS**

1L (32 FL OZ.)

CHICORY
An occasional substitute for coffee, chicory root is a bitter digestive, tonic and purgative. It stimulates the liver, rather like dandelion, which it closely resembles.

DRIED FRUITS
In this drink the dried fruits add a natural sweetness but also contribute their share of minerals, particularly copper for dates, as well as iron, phosphorus and magnesium for dried apricots.

• Pit the dates.
• Cut the dried fruits into small pieces.
• Place all the ingredients together in a jar.
• Leave to infuse for at least 12 hours in the refrigerator before serving.

77

BEETROOT WATER

WITH LEMON & GINGER

PREPARATION TIME **5 MIN**
INFUSION TIME **12 HRS**

250g (9 oz.) beetroot (preferably the Chioggia variety)

3cm (1¼ in.) fresh ginger

1 lemon
* 1l (32 fl oz./1 quart) water

NUTRITIONAL **BENEFITS**

BEETROOT
Beetroot is amongst the vegetables with the highest antioxidant content. They contain betalain, an antioxidant responsible for its dark colour, which has anti-inflammatory properties and stimulates the liver. The skin of a beetroot contains three times more antioxidants than the flesh, so do not peel it.

GINGER
Ginger is a good all-round tonic, it promotes digestion and can even quell the nausea of motion sickness.

1L (32 FL OZ.)

• Slice the beetroot.
• Peel the ginger and slice it into fine strips.
• Peel the lemon and remove all the pith. Cut the lemon into slices.
• Place all the ingredients together in a jar.
• Leave to infuse for at least 12 hours in the refrigerator before serving.

TO USE UP
LEFTOVERS

Use any leftover beetroot and ginger in an Asian-style salad. Prepare a vinaigrette with soy sauce, sesame oil and lemon juice , then add finely chopped Chinese cabbage.

CLEMENTINE WATER
WITH JUNIPER

4 clementines

1 tbsp. juniper berries

juice of 1 whole lemon
+ 1l (32 fl oz./1 quart) water

NUTRITIONAL **BENEFITS**

CLEMENTINE
Like all citrus fruits, clementines are bursting with vitamin C. Due to its beta-cryptoxanthin content, it can help with preventing the loss of calcium from the bones. The antioxidant family of beta-carotene, contained in clementines, is especially effective in postmenopausal women.

JUNPIER
The diuretic properties of junpier berries especially help to relieve gout and any urinary tract infections.

1L (32 FL OZ.)

• Peel and slice the clementines. Set aside the peel of one clementine.
• Coarsely crush the juniper berries with a pestle and mortar, then place them in a muslin bag or ball-shaped tea infuser.
• Place all the ingredients together in a jar.
• Leave to infuse for at least 12 hours in the refrigerator before serving.

LAPACHO WATER

WITH DATES & BLACK PEPPER

PREPARATION TIME **5 MIN**
INFUSION TIME **12 HRS**

2 tbsp. lapacho (or rooibos)

6 Medjool dates (or 9 Deglet Nour dates)

1 tbsp. black peppercorns
+ 1l (32 fl oz./1 quart) water

NUTRITIONAL **BENEFITS**

LAPACHO
Derived from the bark of a tree native to South America, lapacho is free of caffeine and theine. It is known for its antiviral and antibacterial properties, and is good immunity booster.

DATES
Dates are rich in copper, which is central in the formation of collagen and hemoglobin.

BLACK PEPPERCORNS
This everyday spice stimulates digestion and is a good general tonic.

1L (32 FL OZ.)

• Coarsley crush the black peppercorns with a pestle and mortar.
• Pit the dates and cut them into quarters.
• Place the lapacho and crushed peppercorns in a muslin bag or a ball-shaped tea infuser.
• Place all the ingredients together in a jar.
• Leave to infuse for at least 12 hours in the refrigerator before serving.

REINVIGORATING WATER

WITH MANDARIN & PERSIMMON

PREPARATION TIME **5 MIN**
INFUSION TIME **12 HRS**

1 mandarin

2 persimmons

Juice of 1 whole lemon
+ 1l (32 fl oz./1 quart) water

NUTRITIONAL **BENEFITS**

1L (32 FL OZ.)

MANDARIN
Limonoids, the antioxidants found in citrus fruits such as mandarins, have a beneficial effect in the prevention of certain cancers. Similarly, these antioxidants can counteract the onset of osteoporosis.

PERSIMMON
Grown originally in Asia, persimmon is eaten very ripe, almost overripe. It is rich in beta carotene and vitamin C and, like many other fruits and vegetables, it helps to reduce bad cholesterol.

• Slice the persimmon thinly.
• Peel the mandarin then cut into slices. Reserve a small piece of the peel.
• Place all the ingredients together in a jar.
• Leave to infuse for at least 12 hours in the refrigerator before serving.

SOBACHA

FOR DETOXIFICATION

PREPARATION TIME **5 MIN**
INFUSION TIME **12 HRS**

25g (1 oz.) rolled oats

40g (1½ oz.) quinoa

70g (2½ oz.) buckwheat
+ 1l (32 fl oz./1 quart) water

NUTRITIONAL **BENEFITS**

SOBACHA
This is a traditional Japanese drink made of roasted buckwheat (soba means 'buckwheat' and cha means 'tea'). Buckwheat is gluten-free and packed with minerals and vitamin B. It contains at least twice as many antioxidants than most commercial pseudo-cereals.

QUINOA AND OATS
They impart a stronger flavour to the drink and allow you to vary the taste according to your preference, simply adjust the quantities.

1L (32 FL OZ.)

• In a frying pan (skillet), dry toast the oats, quinoa and buckwheat, stirring constantly. The mixture should give off a cookie aroma, without burning.
• Place the toasted grains in a jar and immediately add the water.
• Leave to infuse for at least 12 hours in the refrigerator before serving.

83

AUTUMN WATER

WITH FRESH FIGS
& MUSCAT GRAPES

PREPARATION TIME **5 MIN**
INFUSION TIME **12 HRS**

2 figs

juice of 1 whole lemon
+ 1l (32 fl oz./1 quart) water

225g (8 oz.) muscat grapes
(or other black grapes)

NUTRITIONAL **BENEFITS**

GRAPES
Grapes are a healthy fruit, with many nutritional benefits: they help to safeguard cardiovascular health and are a useful ally in the fight against cancer and other chronic diseases. Black grapes, such as muscat, that are dark in colour are much richer in antioxidants. Grapes are also a good source of manganese and copper.
FIGS
Figs are rich in B vitamins and manganese.

1L (32 FL OZ.)

• Cut the grapes in half.
• Cut the figs into slices.
• Place all the ingredients together in a jar.
• Leave to infuse for at least 12 hours in the refrigerator before serving.
NOTE
With the leftover fruit from this recipe, you can make the sugar-free jam (see page 117).

AN AUTUMNAL ALTERNATIVE
WITH BLACK
GRAPES & PEAR

You can easily
replace the fresh
figs with a small
ripe pear.

BLOOD ORANGE WATER WITH

CRANBERRIES

& ROSEMARY

PREPARATION TIME **5 MIN**
INFUSION TIME **12 HRS**

5 sprigs of rosemary

2 blood oranges

*50g (2 oz.) cranberries
+ 1l (32 fl oz./1 quart) water*

NUTRITIONAL **BENEFITS**

BLOOD ORANGES
This variety of orange, the blood orange, contains anthocyanin, which is the same pigment found in blueberries. In particular, this water-soluble antioxidant plays a key role in cardiovascular health.

CRANBERRIES
This fruit makes an effective natural remedy for urinary infections.

ROSEMARY
Rosemary helps to relieve digestive problems and respiratory infections.

1L (32 FL OZ.)

• Peel the oranges and remove all the pith, then cut the oranges into slices.
• Reserve a small strip of the orange peel.
• Place all the ingredients together in a jar.
• Leave to infuse for at least 12 hours in the refrigerator before serving.

NOTE
For a sweeter tasting drink, use dried cranberries instead of fresh.

AUTUMNAL WATER

WITH BLACK GRAPES

& RED VINE

PREPARATION TIME **5 MIN**
INFUSION TIME **12 HRS**

300g (10½ oz.) black grapes

2 tbsp. dried
red vine leaves

juice of 1 whole lemon

*1l (32 fl oz./1 quart) water

NUTRITIONAL **BENEFITS**

1L (32 FL OZ.)

RED VINE

Dried red vine leaves are traditionally used in herbal medicine to stimulate circulation, helping to prevent varicose veins and reduce edema. It is rich in quercetin, an antioxidant of the flavonoid family. Combined with black grapes, whose skin is rich in resveratrol, another antioxidant, both help to reduce cholesterol, blood pressure and stress.

• Place the red vine leaves in a muslin bag or a ball-shaped tea infuser.
• Cut the grapes in half.
• Place all the ingredients together in a jar.
• Leave to infuse for at least 12 hours in the refrigerator before serving.

GREEN MATE

WITH CHAI SPICES

½ tsp. fennel seeds
2 cinnamon sticks
8 cardamom pods
1 tsp. black peppercorns

5cm (2 in) fresh ginger

1½ tbsp.
green mate

the juice of
1 whole lime
* 1l (32 fl oz./1 quart) water

NUTRITIONAL **BENEFITS**

GREEN MATE
A traditional drink consumed in South America, including Argentina, green mate or yerba mate is used to combat physical and mental fatigue and improve alertness. Indeed, it contains caffeine to stimulate the nervous system.

CHAI SPICES
This mixture of traditional Indian spices consists of cinnamon, ginger, cardamom, fennel and pepper. It lends this drink a warmth that aids the digestion.

1L (32 FL OZ.)

• Peel the ginger and cut it into thin strips.
• In a pestle and mortar, crush the cinnamon sticks, cardamom pods, peppercorns and fennel seeds.
• Place the mate, crushed cinnamon, cardamom, peppercorns and fennel in a muslin bag or ball-shaped tea infuser.
• Place all the ingredients together in a jar.
• Leave to infuse for at least 12 hours in the refrigerator before serving.

ROOIBOS INFUSION WITH

APRICOT & TONKA BEAN

PREPARATION TIME **5 MIN**
INFUSION TIME **12 HRS**

1½ tbsp. rooibos

2 tonka beans

5 dried apricots

1 (32 fl oz/1 quart) water

NUTRITIONAL **BENEFITS**

1L (32 FL OZ.)

ROOIBOS
As it contains no caffeine, rooibos can be drunk by anyone without affecting their sleep.

TONKA BEANS
This spice is reminiscent of both hay and almonds. It is said to have anti-coagulant properties. Be careful not to abuse this spice: it contains coumarin, a substance that is toxic in high doses.

DRIED APRICOTS
A good source of vitamins A, B3 and B5, as well as copper and iron.

• Coarsley crush the tonka beans with a pestle and mortar.
• Put the crushed tonka beans and rooibos in a muslin bag or ball-shaped tea infuser.
• Cut the dried apricots into small pieces.
• Place all the ingredients together in a jar.
• Leave to infuse for at least 12 hours in the refrigerator before serving.

CELERY WATER
WITH APPLE & LIME

PREPARATION TIME **5 MIN**
INFUSION TIME **12 HRS**

2 small apples

60g (2 oz.) celery

1 lime

* 1l (32 fl oz./1 quart) water

NUTRITIONAL **BENEFITS**

APPLE
This ubiquitous fruit contains fibre, vitamins C and K, as well as manganese.

CELERY
Celery contains antioxidants from the polyacetylenes family, which have antibacterial and anti-inflammatory properties. Celery is also a source of vitamins C and K, necessary for blood clotting, and B6, used in the formation of red blood cells.

1L (32 FL OZ.)

• Cut the apples into quarters, remove the core and seeds and chop into small pieces.
• Chop the celery into small pieces.
• Peel the lime and remove the pith. Cut the lime into slices.
• Place all the ingredients together in a jar.
• Leave to infuse for at least 12 hours in the refrigerator before serving.

FOR
ALTERNATIVE
FLAVOURS

This recipe also
works exceptionally
well with pear.

REVITALIZING WATER

WITH PARSNIP & PEAR

PREPARATION TIME **5 MIN**
INFUSION TIME **12 HRS**

150g (5½ oz.) parsnip

2 pears

juice of 1 whole lemon
+ 1l (32 fl oz./1 quart) water

NUTRITIONAL **BENEFITS**

PEARS
The antioxidants in pears have a beneficial effect on blood lipids, especially for smokers. Pears are also a useful source of copper and vitamin C.

PARNSIPS
A cousin of the carrot, parsnips have soft flesh that tastes slightly aniseed in flavour. Parsnips contain polyacetylenes, which are easily digestible and have a preventive effect in the fight against some cancers. This root vegetable is also packed with manganese.

1L (32 FL OZ.)

• Cut the pears into quarters, remove the cores and chop them into pieces.
• Slice the parsnip thinly.
• Place all the ingredients together in a jar.
• Leave to infuse for at least 12 hours in the refrigerator before serving.

BLACK TEA
WITH CLEMENTINE
& CLOVE

PREPARATION TIME **5 MIN**
INFUSION TIME **12 HRS**

2 clementines

1 tbsp.
Darjeeling tea

4 cloves
+ 1 (32 fl. oz./1 quart) water

NUTRITIONAL **BENEFITS**

BLACK TEA
Slightly less rich in polyphenols than green tea, black tea is nevertheless a pleasant caffeinnated drink.
CLEMENTINES
Rich in vitamin C, this citrus fruit helps to prevent heart disease by reducing blood cholesterol levels.
CLOVES
Its toning and anti-inflammatory properties are traditionally used to soothe toothache.

1L (32 FL OZ.)

• Peel the clementines and cut them into thin slices. Reserve one thin strip of peel.
• Coarsely crush the cloves with a pestle and mortar.
• Place the cloves and tea in a muslin bag or ball-shaped tea infuser.
• Place all the ingredients together in a jar.
• Leave to infuse for at least 12 hours in the refrigerator before serving.

SLIMMING WATER

WITH PINK GRAPEFRUIT
& LYCHEES

PREPARATION TIME **5 MIN**
INFUSION TIME **12 HRS**

1 pink grapefruit

juice of 1 whole lemon
+ 1l (32 fl oz./1 quart)
water

300g (10½ oz.) lychees

NUTRITIONAL **BENEFITS**

GRAPEFRUIT
Choose pink or red varieties of grapefruit for their greater antioxidant content. Grapefruit is rich in vitamins C, A and B5, as well as copper. It has anti-inflammatory properties and, when consumed daily, can help to promote weight loss.

LYCHEES
This fruit is rich in minerals, especially potassium, copper and magnesium. The mild, sweet flavour of lychees counteracts the bitterness of the grapefruit.

1L (32 FL OZ.)

• Peel and stone the lychees. Chop into pieces.
• Peel the grapefruit and remove all the pith. Cut the grapefruit into slices.
• Place all the ingredients together in a jar.
• Leave to infuse for at least 12 hours in the refrigerator before serving.

USE CANNED LYCHEES

You can always use canned lychess if you cannot find them fresh. Simply drain the syrup from the fruit and then to remove all traces of sugar, rinse the lychees in running water.

IMMUNITY WATER

WITH EUCALYPTUS

PREPARATION TIME **5 MIN**
INFUSION TIME **12 HRS**

2 tbsp. dried eucalyptus leaves

3 sprigs of dried rosemary

1 tsp. dried thyme +
1l (32 fl oz./1 quart)
water

NUTRITIONAL **BENEFITS**

EUCALYPTUS
Traditionally used in herbal remedies to treat winter ailments, eucalyptus is beneficial for the respiratory system - soothing sore throats and easing bronchitis - and even to help relieve asthma.

ROSEMARY & THYME
These two herbs are a good general tonic, with anti-bacterial properties that can help to protect the ears, nose and throat.

1L (32 FL OZ.)

- Tear the eucalyptus leaves.
- Place all the ingredients together in a jar.
- Leave to infuse for at least 12 hours in the refrigerator before serving.
- Serve with a little lemon and honey, if preferred.

NOTE
Feel free to replace the rosemary with echinacea (available from health food stores). This is very efficient against flu symptoms; take it at the first sign of a chill.

APPLE WATER

WITH CARDAMOM

PREPARATION TIME **5 MIN**
INFUSION TIME **12 HRS**

2 apples

12 cardamom pods

juice of 1 whole lemon
+ 1l (32 fl oz./1 quart) water

NUTRITIONAL **BENEFITS**

APPLES
The antioxidants in apples have a preventive effect against some cancers, including lung cancer and bowel cancer. Some studies also show its positive effect on the respiratory system, including asthma.

CARDAMOM
A good general stimulant, cardamom has anti-bacterial properties and helps to fight sickness and digestive disorders.

1L (32 FL OZ.)

• Cut the apples into quarters, remove the core and seeds, them cut into pieces.
• Open the cardamom pods and crush them gently in their skins with a pestle and mortar. Place in a muslin bag or ball-shaped tea infuser.
• Place all the ingredients together in a jar.
• Leave to infuse for at least 12 hours in the refrigerator before serving.

ACAI WATER

WITH SUPERFRUITS

Juice of 1 whole lemon + 1l (32 fl oz./1 quart) water

25g (1 oz.) goji berries
25g (1 oz.) cranberries
25g (1 oz.) mulberries
(or raisins)

1 tsp. acai powder

NUTRITIONAL **BENEFITS**

SUPERFRUITS

These small superfruits have become highly popular recently, mainly due to their unusual antioxidant properties. Acai, a small berry native to South America, is surprisingly rich in lipids. This is a source of vitamins E and B1, as well as iron. Cranberries are rich in vitamin C and are beneficial to the urinary system. In traditional Chinese medicine, goji berries are believed to be beneficial to the liver and immune system.

1L (32 FL OZ.)

• Place all the ingredients together in a jar and mix to dissolve the acai powder.
• Leave to infuse for at least 12 hours in the refrigerator before serving.

NOTE

This recipe lends itself particularly well to a fizzy version. Replace half the amount of water with sparkling water, which is added after the still water has been infused by the fruit, just before serving.

CRANBERRIES & MULBERRIES

For this recipe, you can use a single variety of superfruit. The tart flavour of cranberries pairs extremely well with the acai. For a sweeter drink, use just mulberries instead.

SQUASH WATER

WITH CHRISTMAS

SPICES

PREPARATION TIME **5 MIN**
INFUSION TIME **12 HRS**

3 star anise

4cm (1½ in.) fresh ginger

300g (10½ oz.) pumpkin flesh

4 cinnamon sticks

juice of 1 whole lemon
+ 1l (32 fl oz./1 quart) water

NUTRITIONAL **BENEFITS**

1L (32 FL OZ.)

PUMPKIN

Autumnal squashes, such as pumpkins, are rich in carotenoids (beta-carotene, zeaxanthin and lutein) that protect the immune system. They are a source of iron, manganese, copper, vitamins C, K , B6 and B9. Pumpkin has a particularly fine and sweet flesh that is ideal in this spicy detox water. The other spices with which the pumpkin is paired have a stimulating and positive effect on the digestive system.

• Cut the pumpkin flesh into pieces.
• Break the cinnamon into two or three pieces, or crush them with a pestle and mortar.
• Chop the ginger into thin slices.
• Put the cinnamon, ginger and star anise in a muslin bag.
• Place all the ingredients together in a jar.
• Leave to infuse for at least 12 hours in the refrigerator before serving.

QUINCE WATER

WITH CHAMOMILE FLOWERS

PREPARATION TIME **5 MIN**
INFUSION TIME **12 HRS**

2 quinces

2 tbsp. dried chamomile flowers

+ juice of 1 whole lemon
1L (32 fl oz./1 quart) water

NUTRITIONAL **BENEFITS**

QUINCE
Quince fruits are a source of vitamin C, which is preserved in this detox water because it is water-soluble. The quince also contains a good amount a potassium, a mineral that helps to balance acid levels in the body and promotes digestion.

CHAMOMILE FLOWERS
Traditionally consumed as an evening tea, chamomile has a calming effect on the digestive system. Feverfew, a less common variety of chamomile, helps to relieve migraines.

1L (32 FL OZ.)

• Wipe the quinces with a clean cloth (do not wash them), then cut into quarters. Remove the hard core and chop the flesh into pieces.
• Put the chamomile flowers in a muslin bag or ball-shaped tea infuser.
• Place all the ingredients together in a jar.
• Leave to infuse for at least 12 hours in the refrigerator before serving.

COFFEE WATER

WITH RAISINS
& CINNAMON

75g (2½ oz.) raisins

15g (½ oz.) coffee beans

3 cinnamon sticks
+ 1l (32 fl oz./1 quart) water

NUTRITIONAL **BENEFITS**

COFFEE
When consumed in moderate amounts, coffee can be beneficial, providing you choose organic beans. Coffee is an antioxidant; it contains caffeine which can improve alertness and athletic performance. According to some recent studies, coffee may have a preventive effect on Parkinson's disease.

RAISINS
They provide a source of iron, phosphorus and potassium.

1L (32 FL OZ.)

• With a pestle and mortar, coarsely crush the coffee beans and cinnamon sticks.
• Put the crushed coffe and cinnamon into a muslin cloth or a ball-shaped tea infuser.
• Place all the ingredients together in a jar.
• Leave to infuse for at least 12 hours in the refrigerator before serving.

AMERICAN-
STYLE LATTE

Use the leftovers
from this coffee-
infused detox water
to make a delicious
hazlenut latte
smoothie (see
recipe on
page 115).

DETOX WATER
WITH EXTRA
VITAMIN C

PREPARATION TIME **5 MIN**
INFUSION TIME **12 HRS**

2 kiwis

1 orange

30g (2 oz.) parsley
+ 1l (32 fl oz./1 quart)
water

NUTRITIONAL **BENEFITS**

VITAMIN C
Vitamin C (or ascorbic acid) plays an important role in immunity, but is also beneficial for healthy bones, teeth and cartilage, as well as promoting healing and iron absorption. Vitamin C is found in high quantities in kiwi fruit, oranges and parsley. While easily destroyed by heat, vitamin C is soluble in water so it works very well in this cold infusion.

1L (32 FL OZ.)

- Peel the kiwis and chop them into pieces.
- Peel the oranges and remove all the pith. Cut the oranges into slices.
- Place all the ingredients together in a jar.
- Leave to infuse for at least 12 hours in the refrigerator before serving.

NOTE
After drinking the detox water, continue to enjoy the fruits by using them to make a smoothie (see recipe on page 111).

EARL GREY TEA
WITH MULBERRIES

PREPARATION TIME **5 MIN**
INFUSION TIME **12 HRS**

65g (2½ oz.) mulberries (or raisins)

1 tbsp. Earl Grey tea

juice of 1 whole lemon + 1l (32 fl oz./1 quart) water

NUTRITIONAL **BENEFITS**

1L (32 FL OZ.)

EARL GREY TEA
A black tea flavoured with bergamot, it is best to buy organic Early Grey to ensure that the bergamot is natural. You can always use green tea rather than black, for its superior antioxidant content if preferred.

MULBERRY
Mulberry is one of the key superfruits (see page 98). This recipe uses the dried fruit of the white mulberry, which is very rich in iron and vitamin C.

• Place the tea in a muslin bag or ball-shaped tea infuser.
• Place all the ingredients together in a jar.
• Leave to infuse for at least 12 hours in the refrigerator before serving.

KOMBUCHA

WITH TROPICAL FRUITS

PREPARATION TIME **5 MIN**
INFUSION TIME **12 HRS**

150g (5½ oz.) pineapple
(2 slices)

1 passion fruit

1 banana
or 150g (5½ oz.) mango

330ml (11 fl oz.) kombucha
+ 600ml (20 fl oz.) water

NUTRITIONAL **BENEFITS**

TROPICAL FRUITS
Tropical fruits are a good source of vitamin C, stimulating the immune system. The passion fruit also helps to prevent the development of cancer cells.

KOMBUCHA
This is a fermented beverage made from bacteria and yeast, traditionally consumed in Russia and China. It is recommended in cases of fatigue and assists in the function of healthy intestinal flora.

1L (32 FL OZ.)

• Peel and slice the banana.
• Chop the pineapple into chunks.
• Cut the passionfruit in half, then scrape out the seeds and pulp.
• Place all the ingredients except the kombucha together in a jar.
• Leave to infuse for at least 12 hours in the refrigerator before serving.
• Add the kombucha then serve immediately.

BANCHA GREEN TEA

WITH ASIAN PEAR

PREPARATION TIME **5 MIN**
INFUSION TIME **12 HRS**

1 tbsp. Japanese bancha tea (see note below)

2 Asian pears

juice of 1 whole lemon
+ 1l (32 fl oz./1 quart) water

NUTRITIONAL **BENEFITS**

BANCHA GREEN TEA
A Japanese roasted green tea, bancha tea contains less caffeine than Sencha green tea. A good quality bancha is a source of various minerals and is otherwise alkalizing.

ASIAN PEARS
Originally from Japan, too, the Asian pear is a cross between a pear and an apple. As well as having cancer-fighting properties, the nashi or Asian pear, is thought to aid recovery from a hangover.

1L (32 FL OZ.)

• Cut the Asian pears into quarters, remove the core and chop the flesh into pieces.
• Place the tea in a muslin bag or a ball-shaped tea infuser.
• Place all the ingredients together in a jar.
• Leave to infuse for at least 12 hours in the refrigerator before serving.

NOTE
Any other Japanese roasted green tea, such as Hojicha or Genmaicha, will work equally well for this recipe.

PAGE 111

PAGE 114

PAGE 1

PAGE 118

PAGE 122

Little
Extras

SMOOTHIES, CHUTNEYS, PANCAKES, PESTO, FLAVOURED ICE CUBES...
HERE ARE SOME IDEAS FOR RECIPES THAT MAKE GOOD USE OF THE
LEFTOVER INGREDIENTS FROM YOUR DETOX WATERS, IN ORDER TO
GET THE FULL BENEFIT OF ALL THEIR NUTRITIONAL PROPERTIES.

SMOOTHIE

WITH RED FRUITS

¼ tsp.
ground cardamom

leftover fruit from Ruby Water with
Mixed Red Fruits & Hibiscus Flowers
(see recipe on page 40), well drained

300ml (10 fl oz) red grape juice

NUTRITIONAL **BENEFITS**

You can safely enjoy macerated hibiscus
flowers as they are perfectly edible and
delicious! Their tartness, due to the vitamin C
they contain, is balanced by the sweetness
of the red grape juice. As an alternative, try
adding hibiscus flowers to a cake batter or
enjoy them with some firm cheeses and a
little honey.

MAKES 2 OR 3 SERVINGS

• Place all the ingredients in a blender and
whizz until smooth.
• Serve immediately.

SMOOTHIE
WITH EXTRA
VITAMIN C

PREPARATION TIME **5 MIN**

½ tsp. ground cinnamon

leftover fruit from Detox Water with Extra Vitamin C (see recipe on page 104), well drained

400ml (13½ fl oz.) fresh orange juice

½ tsp. acerola powder (optional)

NUTRITIONAL **BENEFITS**

Vitamin C is water soluble, which means that the detox water leftovers of kiwi fruit and parsley will be packed with lots of vitamin C. Boost the vitamin C content even further by adding orange juice – ideallyfreshly pressed – and some optional powdered acerola. In addition, you will reap the benefits of hesperidin, a flavonoid present in oranges, especially in its membranes.

MAKES 4 SERVINGS

• Place all the ingredients in a blender and whizz until smooth.
• Serve immediately.
NOTE
Acerola powder (a 98% natural product) can be bought online and in health food stores.

GREEN SMOOTHIE
WITH PEAR

leftover fruit and vegetables from
Pear Water with Fennel & Ginger
(see recipe on page 72), well drained

2 tsp. honey

400ml (13½ fl oz.) pear juice
(or cloudy apple juice)

NUTRITIONAL **BENEFITS**

Adding a small serving of vegetables to a fruit smoothie is an easy way of incorporating healthy vegetable within breakfast. The aniseed flavour of the fennel is a pleasant foil for the pear, plus both are rich in fibre. If you do not want to make the pear juice yourself, opt for an organic pear juice, an apple-pear blend or just apple on its own. Avoid syrups, which contain added sugar.

MAKES 4 SERVINGS

• Place in a blender with the honey and 300ml (10 fl oz.) of the pear juice. Whizz until smooth.
• Add more of the remaining pear juice to achieve the desired consistency.
• Serve immediately.

LATTE-STYLE SMOOTHIE
WITH HAZELNUTS

leftover fruit and spices from
Coffee Water with Raisins &
Cinnamon (see recipe on page 102)

(see recipe on page 102)

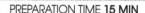

PREPARATION TIME **15 MIN**

500ml (17 fl oz.) soy milk

1 tbsp. maple syrup

for the coconut Chantilly cream
200ml (6¾ fl oz.) coconut cream
(placed in the refrigerator the day before)
ground cinnamon
4 tsp. maple syrup

60g (2 oz.) hazelnut purée

NUTRITIONAL **BENEFITS**

Here is a latte-style smoothie recipe to reuse the macerated coffee beans from the Coffee Water with Raisins & Cinnamon. This is a 100% vegetarian drink that is also dairy free, using soy milk and coconut cream. The coconut Chantilly cream is a classic whipped cream. This delicately perfumed cloud of whipped cream adds a lot of sweetness to the drink.

MAKES 4 SERVINGS

• Pour the coconut cream into a large bowl. Using an electric whisk, whip the coconut cream until fluffy to make the Chantilly. Keep it in a cool place.
• Stir the soy milk and pour it in a blender. Add the detox water residue, hazelnut purée and maple syrup. Whizz until smooth and frothy.
• Pour into a tall glass. Finish with a cloud of coconut Chantilly cream, sprinkle with cinnamon and drizzle with maple syrup.
• Serve immediately.

TROPICAL FRUIT
SMOOTHIE

leftover fruit from Antioxidant Water
with Pomegranate & Banana
(see recipe on page 64), well drained

2 tsp. coconut sugar

250ml (8½ fl. oz.) coconut milk

Juice of 1 lime

¼ tsp. vanilla
powder

NUTRITIONAL **BENEFITS**

Here is a fragrant and creamy smoothie, made with ingredients that evoke the tropical sun. Exotic fruit, coconut milk and lime combine to create a well-balanced flavour. Coconut sugar is a natural sugar made from the sap of the coconut flower. It is rich in minerals, including potassium, and has a low glycemic index. It imparts a delicious caramel flavour.

MAKES 2 OR 3 SERVINGS

• Place all the ingredients in a blender and whizz until smooth.
• Serve immediately.

ADD FRESH
GINGER

For a spicier
flavour, add some
grated fresh ginger
to this lucious
smoothie drink.

PUMPKIN SPICE

SMOOTHIE

leftover squash and spices from Squash Water with Christmas Spices (see recipe on page 100), well drained and the pumpkin and spices separated

2 tsp. honey

400ml (14 fl oz.) almond milk

2 tbsp. white almond purée

juice of 1 whole lemon

NUTRITIONAL **BENEFITS**

As well as a traditional winter soup, squashes make delicious desserts and drinks, especially pumpkin. With this smoothie you can enjoy the fibre, carotenoids and non-soluble antioxidants, where the absorption is optimized thanks to the lipids contained in the almond purée. If you use unsweetened almond milk, you can add an extra teaspoonful of honey.

SERVES 4

• Cook the pumpkin pieces over steam for at least 20 minutes, until soft.
• Place the pumpkin pieces, almond purée, almond milk, honey and lemon juice in a blender. Add one third of the spices, plus 2 or 3 star anise. Whizz all the ingredients together until smooth.
• Check the flavour and add more spices according to taste, then whizz in the blender again. Serve immediately.

SUGAR-FREE JAM

WITH FIGS

& RAISINS

PREPARATION TIME **30 MIN**
RESTING TIME **2 OR 3 HRS**

leftover fruit from Autumn Water
with Fresh Figs and Muscat Grapes
(see recipe on page 84)

1 pinch of ground cinnamon
or vanilla powder

2 tbsp. set honey

30g (1 oz.) chia seeds

NUTRITIONAL **BENEFITS**

Chia seeds are high in fibre, omega-3 and calcium. These tiny seeds absorb a large volume of water to form a gel, which means a raw jam can be made quickly and easily using any leftover fruits from a detox water.

VARIATION

All red and yellow summer fruits (including peaches, apricots, and melons) are highly suitable for this recipe.

350G (12 OZ.) JAR

• Using a knife, deseed the grapes.
• Place the fruit in a blender and whizz in short bursts of 1 or 2 seconds, leaving some of the fruit in larger pieces.
• Stir in the honey, cinnamon and chia seeds, then mix thoroughly.
• Leave to expand for 20 minutes, stir and leave in the refrigerator for several hours to set.

NOTE

Store this jam in the refrigerator and eat within 3 days.

PANCAKES

WITH CARROTS

& SPICES

PREPARATION TIME **10 MIN**
COOKING TIME **8 MIN**

20g (¾ oz.) brown sugar

6 tbsp. soy milk

40g (1½ oz.) brown rice flour

4 eggs
+ 60g (2 oz.) cornstarch
+ 1 tsp. baking powder
+ olive oil or coconut oil (for cooking)

leftover vegetables and spices from
Carrot Cake in a Drink (see recipe on
page 70), well drained

NUTRITIONAL BENEFITS

Pancakes made with vegetable and fruit
purées are an easy way to increase your daily
consumption and hit the recommended 'five-
a-day'. The macerated carrots contain lots of
non-soluble nutrients, so be sure to eat them.
VARIATION
This recipe works well with any leftover
vegetables and fruits (pumpkin, apple, celery,
fennel, parsnip...). However, avoid any
vegetables and fruits that are particularly
watery, such as cucumber, melon and berries.

SERVES 4

• Put the residue of the carrot cake, eggs and
soy milk in a blender. Whizz until you reach a
smooth consistency.
• In a bowl, mix the rice flour, cornstarch, sugar
and baking powder. Gradually stir in the carrot
cake purée.
• Pour several ladlefuls of the batter into a oiled
hot pan. Cook the pancakes for 4–5 minutes
on one side. Flip the pancakes over and then
cook for 3 minutes on the other side. Repeat
with the remaining batter.

VEGETABLE PANCAKES

Using the same basic recipe, make pancakes with other vegetables, such as leftover mashed sweet potatoes or parsnips.

CHUTNEY

WITH LEFTOVER FRUITS

PREPARATION TIME **10 MIN**
COOKING TIME **40 MIN**

leftover fruit from Tonic Water with
Strawberry & Rhubarb (see recipe on
page 43), well drained

½ tsp. salt

1 small red onion

4 tbsp. balsamic vinegar

4 tbsp. cider vinegar

60g (2 oz.) cranberries

4cm (1½ in.) piece of fresh ginger

90g (3 oz.) golden cane sugar

NUTRITIONAL **BENEFITS**

1 SMALL JAR

Feel free to add to this basic recipe a variety of spices, such as cinnamon and cumin, and dried fruits, such as raisins and apricots. At the end of the cooking time, the mixture should be very creamy and all the ingredients have broken down. All fruits and most vegetables are suitable to use in this chutney recipe. But avoid fibrous vegetables, such as carrots or parsnips, for example, which will need to be mashed with a fork.

• Peel and chop the onion into small dice. Peel the ginger and finely chop it into shreds.
• Place all the ingredients into a heavy based saucepan. Cook uncovered over a medium heat for about 40 minutes.
• Transfer the hot chutney to a sterilized jar with a tight fitting lid and leave it to cool completely before sealing the jar.
NOTE
This chutney will keep for several weeks when stored in the refrigerator.

PESTO

WITH THREE HERBS

PREPARATION TIME **10 MIN**

leftover herbs from Garden Herb Water with Lemon (see recipe on page 56), well drained

100ml (3⅓ fl oz.) olive oil

50g (2 oz.) basil leaves

1 garlic clove, crushed

30g (1 oz.) pinenuts

¼ tsp. salt

1 tbsp. lemon juice

NUTRITIONAL **BENEFITS**

Here is an idea to enrich a classic pesto with additional herbs, which pairs well with both vegetables and pasta. This version uses the leftover macerated garden herb leaves of a detox water to impart a different flavour to the pure basil taste of conventional pesto.

VARIATION

You can use other macerated herbs, either a single variety of several types, and mix them with additional fresh herb leaves.

1 SMALL BOWL

• Coarsely chop the leftover garden herb leaves from the detox water and the basil leaves.
• Put all the ingredients in a blender and whizz until smooth.
• Either keep the pesto in the refrigerator and consume within three days or freeze it.

FLAVOURED

ICE CUBES

PREPARATION TIME **5 MIN**
FREEZING TIME **3 HRS MINIMUM**

70g (2½ oz.) berries or other fruit chopped into small pieces + 125ml (4 fl oz.) water

125ml (4 fl oz.) tea (green, white or rooibos) or herbal tea (purifying plant or hibiscus), infused and cooled

40g almonds, puréed + 300ml (10 fl oz.) almond milk

325ml (11 fl oz.) coconut milk

MAKES 12–20 ICE CUBES

FRUIT ICE CUBES
• Divide the fruit between the individual moulds of an ice cube tray and cover with water.
• Freeze for several hours until frozen.

ALMOND MILK ICE CUBES
• Place the almond purée in a bowl then gradually dilute it with the amond milk.
• Pour the milk into the individual moulds of an ice cube tray and freeze for several hours until frozen.

TEA OR HERBAL TEA ICE CUBES
• Pour the cooled tea or herbal tea into the individual moulds of an ice cube tray and freeze for several hours until frozen.

COCONUT MILK ICE CUBES
• Vigorously whisk the coconut milk.
• Pour the milk into the individual moulds of an ice cube tray and freeze for several hours until frozen.

Prepare refreshing ice cubes all year round and enjoy seasonal fruits and spices for optimal nutrition. Fruit ice cubes complement any type of drink: lemonade, fruit juices, even a glass of martini.

INDEX OF RECIPES

IN ALPHABETICAL ORDER

INDEX BY INGREDIENT

CONVERSION TABLE FROM METRIC TO IMPERIAL

WEIGHT	55g	100g	150g	200g	250g	300g	500g	750g	1kg
	2 oz.	3½ oz.	5½ oz.	7 oz.	9 oz.	10½ oz.	17½ oz.	26¼ oz.	35 oz.

For ease of measuring, the equivalent conversions have been rounded up to the nearest quarter of an ounce (28g = 1 oz.).

VOLUMES	50ml	100ml	150ml	200ml	250ml	500ml	750ml
	12/3 fl oz.	31/3 fl oz.	5 fl oz.	6¾ fl oz.	8½ fl oz.	17 onces	251/3 fl oz.

For ease of measuring, one cup is the equivalent of 250ml (1 cup = 8 fl oz. = 230ml).

First published in 2016 by Larousse
This English paperback edition published in 2017 by Quadrille Publishing

First published in 2016 by
Quadrille Publishing Limited
Pentagon House
52–53 Southwark Street
London SE1 1UN
www.quadrille.co.uk
www.quadrille.com

Quadrille is an imprint of Hardie Grant
www.hardiegrant.com.au

British Library Cataloguing-in-Publication Data. A catalogue record for this book is available from the British Library.

ISBN: 978 1 84949 984 2

Printed in Italy

Publishing Directors: Isabelle Jeuge-Maynart & Ghislaine Stora
Editorial Director: Agnès Busiere
Editor: Emilie Franc
Designer: Claire Morel-Fatio
Production: Donia Faiz

For the English language hardback edition:
Publishing Director: Sarah Lavelle
Commissiong Editor: Lisa Pendreigh
Creative Director: Helen Lewis
Designer: Gemma Hayden
Production Director: Vincent Smith
Production Controller: Emily Noto